782.14   Stardust.
STA

$35.00

DATE			

Design for Stardust costume by Erté

STARDUST

Music
from the Broadway show
Produced by Louise Westergaard and Irving Schwartz

Lyrics by
Mitchell Parish

Costumes and theater designs by
Erté

Introduction by PEGGY LEE

Foreword by Erté

Preface by Mitchell Parish

Edited, designed, and produced by Marshall Lee

Harry N. Abrams, Inc.

Publishers, New York

The materials in this book based on the show *Stardust*
are from the Louise Westergaard production

Library of Congress Cataloging-in-Publication Data

Stardust: music for great song hits of the 1920s–50s.

Sheet music of the songs in the musical revue
Stardust.
1. Revues.   2. Popular Music.   I. Parish, Mitchell.
II. Stardust (Revue)
M1503.S7964 1990   90-30345
ISBN 0-8109-3810-3
ISBN 0-8109-2456-0 (pbk.)
ISBN 0-89898-554-4 (Belwin pbk.)

Photo credits: page 8 — photo Samuel S. Teicher; page 10 — photo Bruce Boyajan, courtesy Trump Castle;
page 12 — photo Bob McKinley; page 41 — photo Rolland Shreves;
pages 27, 41, 63, 91, 117 — photos courtesy Frank Driggs

CONTENTS

The names under song titles are the composers.
All lyrics are by Mitchell Parish

1930s

1940s

1950s

MITCHELL PARISH

PREFACE

by MITCHELL PARISH

In many of my song lyrics I've written about dreams. I had my own dreams of glory when I began my career as a budding young songwriter fresh from the Lower East Side of Manhattan. I served my apprenticeship plugging the songs of other, more established writers, singing them in neighborhood movie houses and beer gardens and at picnic grounds, until I finally graduated to writing my own songs. But I never dreamed that one day a Broadway show would feature over thirty songs with my lyrics alone, and that these songs would be the content of a book published by a top art book publisher. There have been shows with the work of only one composer and many lyricists (like Duke Ellington's *Sophisticated Ladies*), but, so far as I know, *Stardust* is the first with only one lyricist and many composers.

Looking back at a long career beginning on that mythical street called Tin Pan Alley, I have no regrets about the path I took. Popular songs, as distinct from show or movie songs, have to stand on their own two little feet, without the support of a story or a grand production. Writing lyrics for songs that millions sing and remember is a challenge and a joy. I am delighted that this book will bring these songs to many people for whom they are cherished memories, and to others for whom they will be a new source of pleasure.

Mitchell Parish

ERTÉ with actress/singer Helen Schneider wearing Stardust costume

FOREWORD
by ERTÉ

My work in graphics, sculpture, fashion, and many other fields of art — as well as the years of World War II — has kept me from designing for Broadway theater for much too long. I loved the opportunity to create costume and set designs for Louise Westergaard's production of *Stardust*, and I am thrilled to have my drawings collected in this beautiful book. So many of the songs in the show were popular in France, and they bring back wonderful memories of the music halls of Paris, London, and Monte Carlo. Of course, musical theater has always been an important part of my life. I have designed for every kind, from the Folies-Bergère and *George White's Scandals* to the Glyndebourne Opera. In fact, among my first costumes was one I created for the tragic Mata Hari in 1913. Besides *Stardust*, I designed for the Radio City Music Hall Easter show in 1990, and I hope to do more designs for the theater in America, where so many people collect my original designs, serigraph prints, sculpture, and objets d'art, as well as the beautiful books that have been published on my work.

MISS PEGGY LEE

INTRODUCTION

by PEGGY LEE

When Marshall Lee (the editor/producer of this book and not a relative) asked that I write this introduction I truly felt honored, because I had seen his fine work. (Although, when he called, a book of mine was on the nonfiction best-seller list in the London *Times*, it's appearance was then so recent that it couldn't have been the reason I was asked.) Then I learned that the work of one of my idols was illustrating *Stardust*, and I was really moved. I have loved Erté as you have for many, many years. His work is truly classic, and there is no one else like him.

I gave the idea a little more thought and realized that I come to this subject not only as a singer but also as a writer of lyrics, so I understand the creative process of writing words for music as well as the pleasurable emotions a singer feels when the words shine and one sees pictures and the rhymes roll around on the tongue like Belgian chocolate. You might say that I have a keen appreciation for lyrics such as these of Mitchell Parish, especially when they float on such grand melodies:

> *When the deep purple falls*
> *over sleepy garden walls*
> *and the stars begin to flicker*
> *in the sky . . .*

I'll always remember when I first heard that song — and I wasn't even in love.

And Mr. Parish manages to breathe life into a stone, as in "Carolina Rolling Stone." You really feel empathy. Then to watch the "Riverboat Shuffle." The lines: *that slide pipe tooter is grand* and, *Mister Hawkins on the tenor* conjure up an era of joy and humor. *Even Mama Dinah will be there to strut for the boys in a room full of noise.* Perfect.

There is something wonderfully implicit in his lyrics—you feel you are experiencing something extra, a double entendre, that is. To remember whatever happened "One Morning in May". . . there is a certain mystique. Or what that "Sentimental Gentleman from Georgia" whispered in your ear.

And "Sweet Lorraine." I first heard that song about 1939, when the beloved Nat "King" Cole was performing at a little place in Los Angeles called the Fox Hills Studio Club. Mostly he played the piano, so it was a double treat to hear that wonderful voice singing those wonderful words:

> *Just found joy*
> *I'm as happy as*
> *a baby boy*
> *with another brand new*
> *choo choo toy*

"Sophisticated Lady" expresses the essence of many women's lives. A lot of us have identified with it. I know I have.

> *They say into your early life*
> *romance came*
> *and in this heart of yours*
> *burned a flame*
> *A flame that flickered*
> *one day and died—*
> *away . . .*

And a man, hearing the same message, feels compassion for the woman. A sad thought but a true one. Song lyrics are a form of poetry that can distill a story. For instance, this one is a whole script; it's a short story all in one song.

> *Then with disillusion deep*
> *in your eyes*
> *You learned that fools in love*
> *soon grow wise*
> *The years have changed you, somehow—*
> *I see you now . . .*

That is why lyrics are such a powerful form of communication.

> *. . . Smoking—drinking*
> *never thinking of*
> *tomorrow—nonchalant*
> *Diamonds shining, dancing,*
> *dining with some man*
> *in a restaurant*
> *Is that all you really want?*

And then, the end:

> *No, sophisticated lady; I know*
> *you miss the love you lost*
> *long ago*
> *And when nobody is nigh—*
> *You cry*

I haven't said much about the music. It's all lovely, like "Stairway to the Stars." And then there is a spot of humor with "Wealthy, Shmelthy, as Long as You're Healthy." Milton Berle used it and set off a national fad.

Now we come into the 1930s. Studs Terkel, in his book *Hard Times*, called them the "dirty thirties." During that depression, songs brightened up our world, songs like "Sidewalks of Cuba" from the Cotton Club Parade of 1935. Lena Horne was then just a mere child in the chorus, but she was so outstanding that they gave her the lead. At that time I was still in North Dakota, falling in love to "Deep Purple." Beautiful songs do have a way of making you fall in love.

"Moonlight Serenade." I *really* fell in love to this one, with a flying tiger. . . and then he flew away. We danced at a little chicken place in Washington, D.C., where Glenn Miller's band played on the jukebox. The war was starting, and everybody fell in love. You always felt you might never see him again. Now, as I think of it, I still hear the song and I see his face. I'm sure you have one of those memories too.

We long for peace and the end of violence. We need romance for our souls. So we should be watching, hearing and seeing beauty. Hearing and seeing things that make us laugh and smile. We need to hold each other and dance. In other words. . . we need love. I think you'll find the way to all of this with the stardust that is sprinkling on you even now.

Here's to Mitchell Parish and all of the wonderful composers!

Here's to Erté!

And here's to you!

Peggy Lee

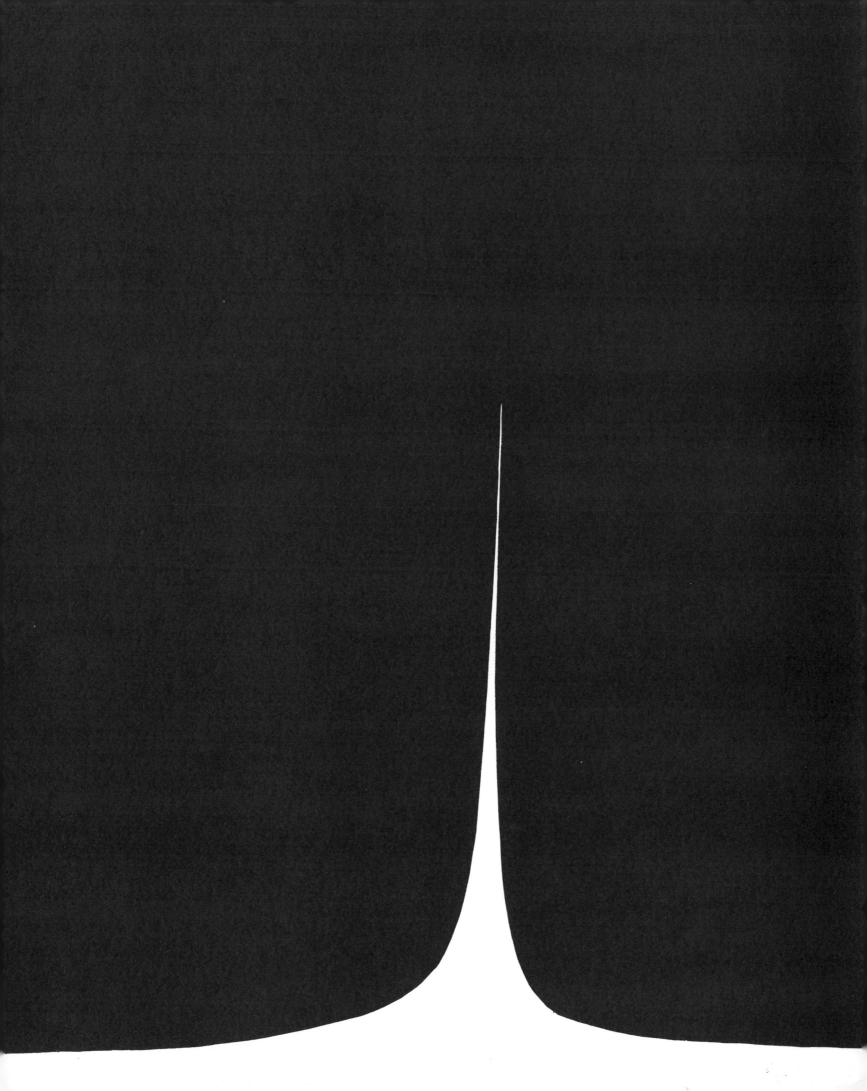

Carolina Rolling Stone

Music by ELEANOR YOUNG, HARRY D. SQUIRES

Poor—— lit-tle me,—— I'm just a Ca-ro-li-na Roll-ing Stone.——

I—— want to be—— with the folks I call my own.—— It seems the

Carolina Rolling Stone

fields of snow-y white _____ are call-ing me to-night,

_____ and I can see my dear old mam-my waiting by the win-dow

light. Down _____ in my heart _____ there is a

pain that nev-er lets me rest. _____ Why _____ did I start

Carolina Rolling Stone

_____ from the ones I love the best?_____ I get so home-sick now and then.

_____ I'll soon be roll-ing home a-gain,_____ be-cause I'm

al - ways alone._____ I'm just a Caro-li-na roll ing stone._____

Fine

Marched my way thro' Geor gia, Miss-is sip-pi, too. Got the trave lin' fe ver

Carolina Rolling Stone

so I blew_ down to Lou'si an- a. Stayed a while and then_ those feet of mine start

walk-in' a-gain._ Been to Al-a-bam-y, sun-ny Ten- nes- see. What's

good e-nough for Mam my_ is good e-nough for me. Bought a one way tick-et.

D.C. al Fine

Leave to-night at nine,_ for I must state the best- est state is Ca- ro-line._

Curtain: "American Indian Dagger Dance": *George White's Scandals*, New York, 1928

Riverboat Shuffle

Music by HOAGY CARMICHAEL, DICK VOYNOW, IRVING MILLS

Good peo - ple, you're in - vit - ed to - night to the Riv - er - boat Shuf - fle! Good peo - ple, we got rhy - thm to - night at the Riv - er - boat Shuf - fle! They tell__ me that

Riverboat Shuffle

slide - pipe toot - er is grand, best in Lou' - si - a - na; So bring your freight - er, come and al - li - ga - tor that band. Mis - ter Hawk - ins on the ten - or! Good peo - ple, you'll hear Mil - len-berg Joys in a spec - ial orch - es - tra - tion!

Riverboat Shuffle

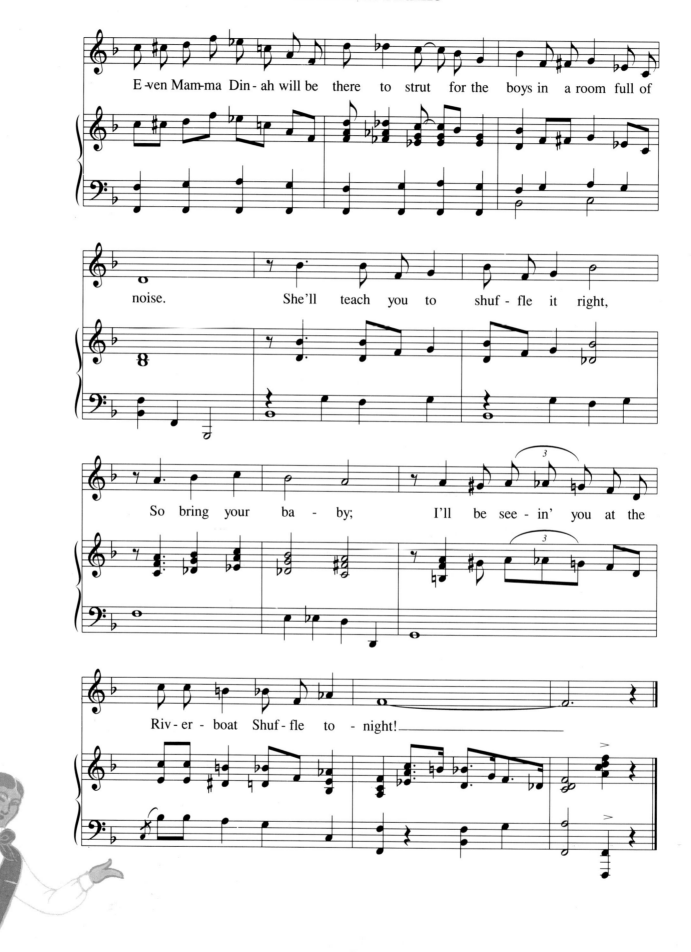

E - ven Mam-ma Din - ah will be there to strut for the boys in a room full of noise. She'll teach you to shuf - fle it right, So bring your ba - by; I'll be see - in' you at the Riv - er - boat Shuf - fle to - night!

HOAGY CARMICHAEL

One Morning in May

Music by HOAGY CARMICHAEL

One morn ing in May, don't for - get, dear, that one won-der-ful

day when we met, dear. The world o - ver was blue

clov - er and hearts, care-free and gay. One

One Morning in May

morn-ing in May, Oh, the rap ture! To-night, dar ling, I pray to re-

capture just one ho-ur, just one flow-er from love's

fad - ed bouqu-et. Kiss - es that came with the

flame of spring - time burn - ing your name in my heart.

One Morning in May

Pre-cious to me like a ros-ar-y, now that we're a-part._____ One morning in May to re-mem-ber. Tho' love smoulders a-way to an ember and dreams perish, we'll still cher-ish that one morn-ing in May._____

One Morning in May

Pale cheeks so soft and white, where do you dream to-night?___ May - be we'll meet a - gain some day, sweet - heart.___

Sweet Lorraine

Music by CLIFF BURWELL

I've just found joy._____ I'm as hap - py as a

ba - by boy_____ with an - oth - er brand new choo - choo toy_____

when I'm with my sweet Lor - raine._____ A

Sweet Lorraine

pair of eyes_____ that are blu - er than the sum - mer skies._____

When you see them you will re - a - lize_____ why I love my sweet Lor-

raine.   (I'm so hap - py.)   When it's rain - ing I don't

miss the sun;   for it's in my sweet - ie's smile,_____

Sweet Lorraine

just to think that I'm the luck-y one who will lead her down the aisle._

_____ Each night I pray_____ that no-bo-dy steals her

heart a-way._____ Just can't wait un-til that hap-py day___

when I mar-ry sweet Lor - raine._____

Costume, "Georgie": *American Millionairess*, Femina Theater, Paris, 1917

Sentimental Gentleman from Georgia

Music by FRANK PERKINS

Hey, hey! No doubt you've heard a -
bout the sweet - est man in Dix - ie - land.
I'll say he's hot. He's got just

Sentimental Gentleman from Georgia

what it takes to make a la - dies man.

When he struts a - long he swings a cane.

Hus - bands tie their wives up with a ball and chain. He's just a

sen - ti - men - tal gen - tle - man from Geor - gia,

Sentimental Gentleman from Georgia

Geor - gia.— Gen - tle to the la - dies all— the time.—

And when it comes— to lov - in' he's a real— prof -fes - sor.—

Yes sir!— Just a Ma - son Dix - on val - en - tine.—

Oh, see those Geor - gia peach - es hang - in' a - round him

Sentimental Gentleman from Georgia

now. 'Cause what this ba-by teach-es no-bo-dy else knows

how. That sen-ti-men-tal gen-tle-man— from Geor-gia,—

Geor - gia.— Gen-tle to the la-dies all— the

time.———— He's just a time.————

DUKE ELLINGTON

Sophisticated Lady

Music by DUKE ELLINGTON, IRVING MILLS

They say_____ in-to your ear-ly life ro-mance came,_____ and in that heart of yours burned a flame._____ A flame that flick-ered one day and died a-

Sophisticated Lady

way.   Then,___ with dis - il - lu - sion deep   in   your

eyes,___ you learned that   fools   in   love soon grow   wise.___ The years have

changed you some- how;   I   see you now.....

Smok - ing, drink- ing, ne -   ver think - ing of to - mor row.___

Sophisticated Lady

Non cha lant. Dia - monds shin - ing, danc - ing, din - ing with some

man in a rest-au-rant. Is that all you real-ly want? No.__ Soph-is-ti-

cat - ed la - dy, I know__ you miss the love you lost long a-

go,__ and when no - bo-dy is nigh you cry.__

Dixie After Dark

Music by BEN OAKLAND, IRVING MILLS

Think of ev'ry- thing that's nice. Add a slice of par-a dise. Mul- ti ply it

all by twice: That's Dix ie af ter dark. If you like your chicken fried,

with the trimmins glori fied and a julep by your side: That's Dixie af ter dark.

Dixie After Dark

Wag - on rides by the light of the moon, head o - ver heels in hay.

Spir-its rise to the height of the moon, liv-in' and lov-in' the night away.

When a voice that gai - ly sings to the twang of ban - jo strings

lends your heart a pair of wings: That's Dixie aft - er dark.

STAIRWAY TO THE STARS

LYRIC BY
MITCHELL PARISH

MUSIC BY
MATT MALNECK
FRANK SIGNORELLI

Featured by
ELEANOR LANE

ROBBINS MUSIC CORPORATION
799 SEVENTH AVENUE · NEW YORK

Stairway to the Stars

Music by MATT MALNICK, FRANK SIGNORELLI

Let's build a stair-way to the stars,

and climb that stair-way to the stars with love be-side us, to

fill the night with a song. We'll hear the

Stairway to the Stars

sound of vi-o-lins out yon-der where the blue be-gins.

The moon will guide us as we go drift-ing a - long.

Can't we sail a-way on a la-zy dai-sy pet-al o-ver the rim of the

hill? Can't we sail a-way on a lit-tle dream and set-tle

Stairway to the Stars

high on the crest of a thrill? Let's build a

stair - way to the stars; a love - ly stair - way to the stars.

It would be heav-en to climb to heav - en with you.

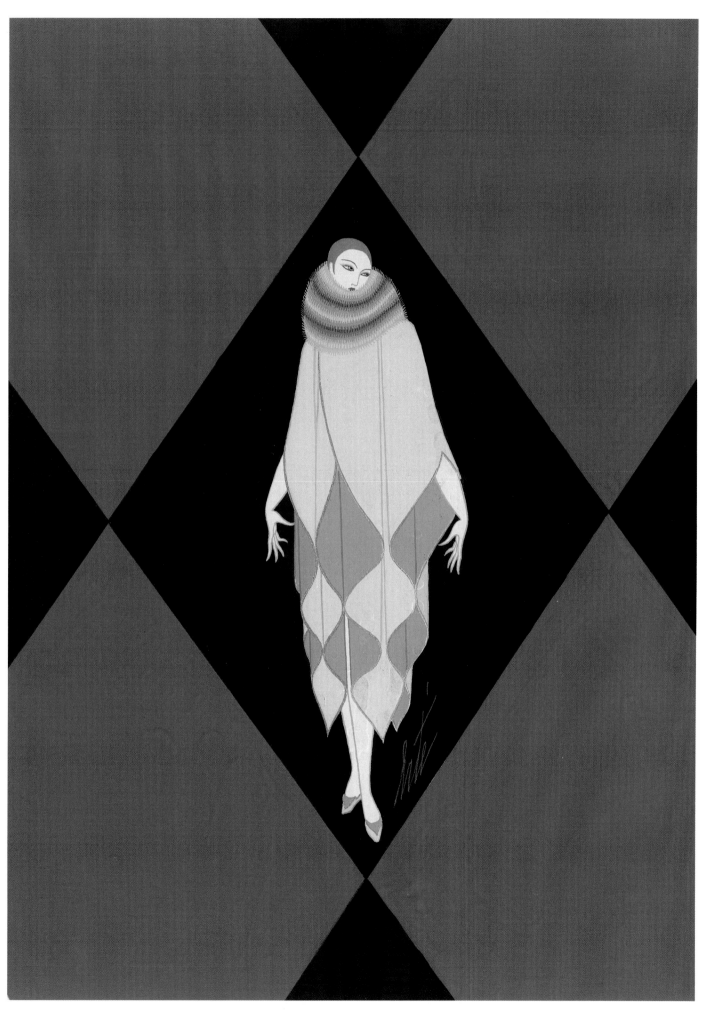

Costume III: *Manhattan Mary*, Majestic Theater, New York, 1927

Wealthy, Shmelthy, As Long as You're Healthy

Music by SAMMY FAIN

If you've got your bread and but-ter, and a

suit of clothes to wear;____ wealth-y shmelth-y, as

long as you're health-y broth-er you're a mil-lion-aire.____ If the

Wealthy, Shmelthy, as Long as You're Healthy

stock that you've been hold-ing   is - n't worth a dime a share;——

wealth - y shmelth - y,   as   long as you're health - y,

broth-er don't you give a care.——   The   best things in life are free:——   the

sun and the moon a - bove.   You   don't   need the   treas-ur - y——

Wealthy, Shmelthy, as Long as You're Healthy

to fall in love. If you've got a lit- tle sweet- ie and she

tells you that it's "yeah";_____ wealth- y shmelth- y as

long as you're health- y, broth- er you're a mil- lion- aire._____

Hands Across the Table

Music by JEAN DELETTRE

Din-ner is end-ed, the mus- ic is grand.

Soft - ly the lan - terns gleam._____ Is - n't it splen - did to

sit hand in hand, si - lent - ly lost in a dream?

Hands Across the Table

Hands a-cross the ta-ble, while the lights are low. Tho' you

hush your lips, your fin-ger-tips tell me all I want to know.

Hands a-cross the ta-ble meet so ten-der-ly, and they

say, in their lit-tle way, that you be-long to me.

You're So Indiff'rent

Music by SAMMY FAIN

You're so in-diff'rent.___ You're so in-diff'rent to me___
so ne-glect-ful.___ It makes me pain-ful-ly blue,___

If you could on-ly learn to love me___ how diff'rent things would be___ You're
to think you think so lit-tle of me,___ the way you seem to do.___

Your en-thu-si-as-im car-ries peo-ple a-way___

You're So Indiff'rent

that's one thing I have learned.__ Is-n't it a pit-y you're sor ta bla sé__

where-ev-er I'm con- cerned. You're so in - diff'rent__

so in- depend ent ly free.__ Tho' I pre sent you with my heart__

most an y one can see__ that you're so in - diff'rent to me.__

It Happens to the Best of Friends

Music by RUBE BLOOM

Why do you try__ to al - i - bi?__ My

heart ful-ly com-prehends,____ though we must say goodbye,__ let's have a

gay good-bye.__ It hap-pens to the best of friends.____ If

It Happens to the Best of Friends

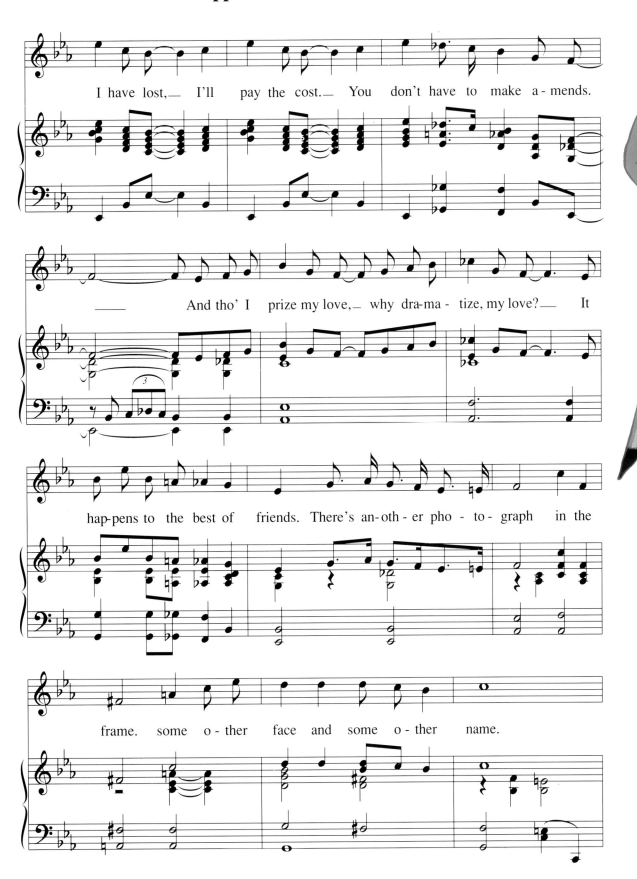

I have lost,— I'll pay the cost.— You don't have to make a-mends.

— And tho' I prize my love,— why dra-ma - tize, my love?— It

hap-pens to the best of friends. There's an-oth-er pho - to- graph in the

frame. some o - ther face and some o -ther name.

It Happens to the Best of Friends

With a smile on my lips I'll shut the door and leave the way I came.___ So take my hand___ and shake my hand,___ and that's how the whole thing ends.___ Don't pi-ty me that way;___ it had to be that way.___ It hap-pens to the best of friends.___

I Would If I Could but I Can't

Music by BING CROSBY, ALAN GREY

Each time you break my heart in two,— I swear with love I'm
Each time you hurt me I for- give.— You're why I want to

through.— And tho' I know it's time I should go.— I would— if I could,—but I
live.— I re- alize I ought to be wise.— I

can't.

would— if I could,— but I can't.

I Would If I Could but I Can't

No ma-gic art and nothing un-der the sun could do what you've done to me.

Al-tho' my heart is breaking you're still the one, and I love you so tender - ly.

It seems as tho' I wor ship you.— no mat ter what you do.—

And that is why I can't say good bye.— I would— if I could, but I can't.

SIDEWALKS OF CUBA

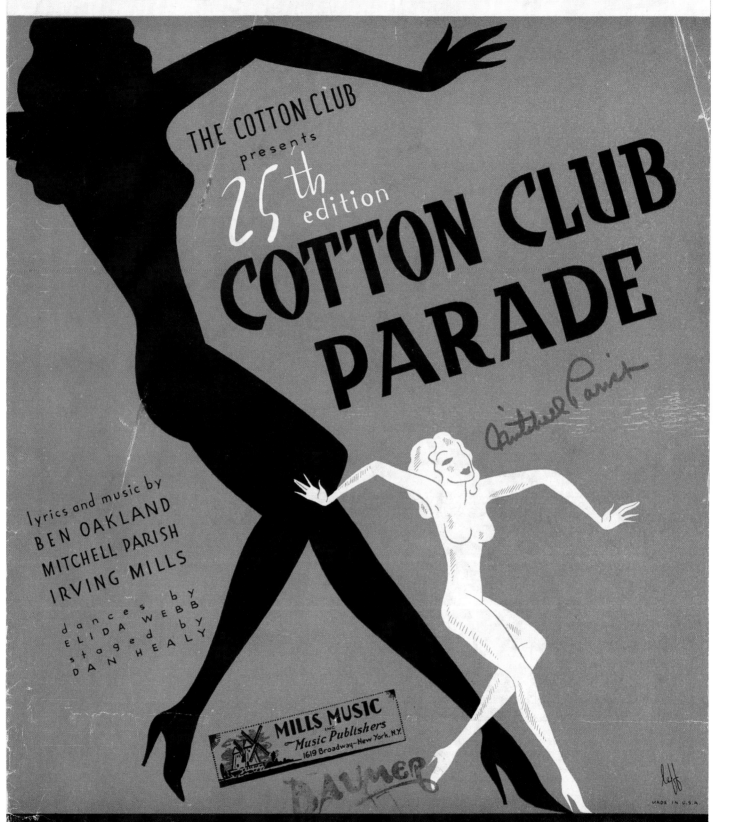

THE COTTON CLUB
presents
25th edition

COTTON CLUB PARADE

lyrics and music by
BEN OAKLAND
MITCHELL PARISH
IRVING MILLS

dances by
ELIDA WEBB
staged by
DAN HEALY

MILLS MUSIC
INC
Music Publishers
1619 Broadway—New York, N.Y.

MADE IN U.S.A.

LIKE A BOLT FROM THE BLUE • SIDEWALKS OF CUBA
I'M A HUNDRED PERCENT FOR YOU • DIXIE AFTER DARK
JINGLE OF THE JUNGLE • RIDIN' HIGH

Sidewalks of Cuba

Music by BEN OAKLAND, IRVING MILLS

Give me a ta-ble for two where we can both sit and view a

sky of blue in a ca-fé, out on the gay side walks of

Cu-ba. And as we sit there and dine, you lift a

Sidewalks of Cuba

Sidewalks of Cuba

(What a band!) I know I'd e-ven go through a re-vo-lu-tion or two, and

so would you._____ I'd take a chance so we could

dance, kiss and ro-mance_____ in a ca-fé,_____

out on the gay_____ side-walks of Cu-ba._____

Evenin'

Music by HARRY WHITE

We were side by side in the eve-nin'— not so ver-y long a-go.

Now I want to hide from the eve nin',— but where, oh where, can I go?

Eve nin',— ev'-ry night you come and you find me,— Must you al-ways come and re-

Evenin'

mind me— that my man is gone?_____ Hur-ry

Eve nin',— can't you see I'm deep in your power.— Ev'-ry min-ute seems like an

ho-ur— since my man is gone,_____

Shadows fall— on the wall,— That's the time that I miss his kiss most of all.

Evenin'

E- ven though I try, how can I go on?—————— Take me,

Eve- nin',— Let me sleep 'til gray dawn is break- in',—

I don't care if I don't a- wak- en,— 'cause my man is

1 gone. **2** gone.————

rit. *pp*

DEEP PURPLE

MUSIC BY
Peter De Rose

LYRIC BY
MITCHELL PARISH

Featured by
JOE VENUTI
and his Orchestra

ROBBINS MUSIC CORPORATION
799 SEVENTH AVENUE · NEW YORK

Deep Purple

Music by PETE DEROSE

The sun is sin-king low be-hind the hill.

I loved you long a-go. I love you still.

A-cross the years you come to me at twi - light

Deep Purple

to bring me love's old thrill. When the deep pur-ple falls o-ver sleep-y gar-den walls, and the stars be-gin to flick-er in the sky, thru the mist of a mem-o-ry you wan-der back to me, breath-ing my name with a sigh.

Deep Purple

In the still of the night once a - gain I hold you tight. Tho' you're

gone your love lives on when moon-light beams._____ And as

long as my heart will beat, lov - er, we'll al-ways meet

here in my deep pur-ple dreams._____

The Scat Song

Music by FRANK PERKINS, CAB CALLOWAY

Man - y words in Web - ster's dic - tion -

ar - y _____ are so ver - y, ver - y or - di -

nar - y, _____ If you can't ex - press your thoughts in

The Scat Song

that way, You can al-ways do it in the

scat way: What's the good in sigh-in' when you're

down in the mouth and blue, Just skat-'n' skeet-'n'

hi de hi, and skat-tle at-tle at da doo,_____ Don't start "me oh

The Scat Song

my - in," it's the worst thing that you can do, Just

skat- 'n' skeet- 'n' hi de hi, and skat - tle at - tle at da doo,—

— Say keep on blow - in' rings and make be -

lieve its a dream,— When you wake up things won't be as

The Scat Song

tough as they seem,___ Tho' you think you're dy-in', there's a

long life a-head of you, Just skat-'n' skeet-'n'

hi de hi, and skat-tle at - tle at da doo.___ doo.

Sophisticated Swing

Music by WILL HUDSON

Sophisticated Swing

Swing._____ There'll be an or-ches-tra play-ing the lat-est hits,_____

While we are swinging and swaying down at the Ritz,_____ Do-in' a per-fect-ly mat-ed So-

phis- ti - ca -ted Swing._____ Mind, we must dance re - fined,

Still if you're in - clined to go to town, we'll go, dear,

Sophisticated Swing

Hon-ey we're gon-na go to it in style de-luxe— And we can just a-bout do it on

sev-en bucks,— Do-in the new-ly cre-a-ted So - phis-ti - ca-ted

1
Swing.——

2
Swing.——

SOPHISTICATED SWING

Music by
WILL HUDSON

Words by
MITCHELL PARISH

MILLS MUSIC
INC
Music Publishers
1619 Broadway-New York, N.Y.

Midnight at the Onyx

Music by WILL HUDSON

All you cranks and all you chron-ics   Throw a-way your pills and

"Jam-min'" is the best ex-press-ion   Of the mu-si-cal pro-

ton-ics,   Spend a mid-night at the On-yx   And

fess-ion;   Just one swing-ing lit-tle sess-ion   Will

get in-to the swing of things.

lift you like a pair of wings.

Midnight at the Onyx

Wah - dah!— Wah - dah!— Show your hon-ey you're a man a-bout town;

Wah - dah!— Wah - dah!— Let her lis- ten to a less-on in sound.—

You'll see swank-y Phil-har-mon ics Rub - bing el- bows with the Bronnix;

Ev - 'ry mid-night at the Onyx They get in-to the swing of things.—

Set. "Conte Hindou": Folies Bergère, Paris, 1922

Tell Me Why

Music by MICHAEL EDWARDS, SIGMUND SPAETH

Tell___ me why___ the stars do shine, Tell___ me
Be - cause God made___ the stars to shine, Be - cause God

why___ the I - vy twines. Tell___ me why___ the
made___ the I - vy twine. Be - cause God made___ the

skies are blue, And I will tell you why I___ love you. you.
skies so blue, That is the rea son why I___ love

Stars Fell on Alabama

Music by FRANK PERKINS

We lived our lit-tle dram a, we kissed in a field of white, and stars fell on Al-a-bama last night, I can't forget the glamour, your eyes held a ten-der light, and stars fell on Al-a-ba-ma last night, I nev-er

Stars Fell on Alabama

planned in my im-a-gi-na-tion— a sit-u- a-tion— so hea-ven-ly,— A fair-y

land where no one else could en-ter,— and in the cen-ter— just you and me, dear,

My heart beat like a ham-mer, my arms wound a-round you tight, and

stars fell on Al- a- ba-ma last night. night.—

BENNY GOODMAN

Don't Be That Way

Music by BENNY GOODMAN, EDGAR SAMPSON

Don't cry, Oh hon-ey please Don't Be That Way,

Clouds in the sky should nev-er make you feel that

way,_____ The rain

Don't Be That Way

will bring the vi - o - lets of May,_____ Tears are in

vain, So hon - ey, please Don't Be That Way,_____ As

long as we____ see it thru,____

You'll have me____ I'll have you,____ Sweet -

93

Don't Be That Way

Organ Grinder's Swing

Music by IRVING MILLS, WILL HUDSON

Who's that com-ing down the street? Good old or-gan grind-er Pete.
Drop a nick-el in his hat Like a rich a - ris - to - crat,

He's the lat-est rhy-thm king with his Or-gan Grind-er's Swing. Da-dya,—
Ev - 'ry nick-el that you fling makes that or-gan grind-er swing. Hi-ho,—

Pa swings it,— so does ma,— Ma swings it,— so does pa,— You swing it,—

Da dya,_____ Da dya,_____
Hi ho,_____ Hi ho,_____

Organ Grinder's Swing

Organ Grinder's Swing

All the chil-dren tag a-long,   Just to lis-ten   to his song,
Do we get a   lot-ta thrills,   Lean-ing on our   win-dow sills,

Mon-key danc-ing   on a string   to the Or-gan   Grind-er's Swing. O-hum,—
List-'ning to a   catch-y thing   like the Or-gan   Grind-er's Swing. Da-dya,—

Pa— swings it,—   so does ma,—   Ma— swings it,-   so does pa,—

O-hum,————————————— O-hum,-
Da-dya,———————————— Da-dya,—

You— swing it,—   so do I.—   I— swing it,—   so do you.—

O-hum,————————
Da-dya,—

MOONLIGHT SERENADE

LYRIC BY
MITCHELL PARISH
MUSIC BY
GLENN MILLER

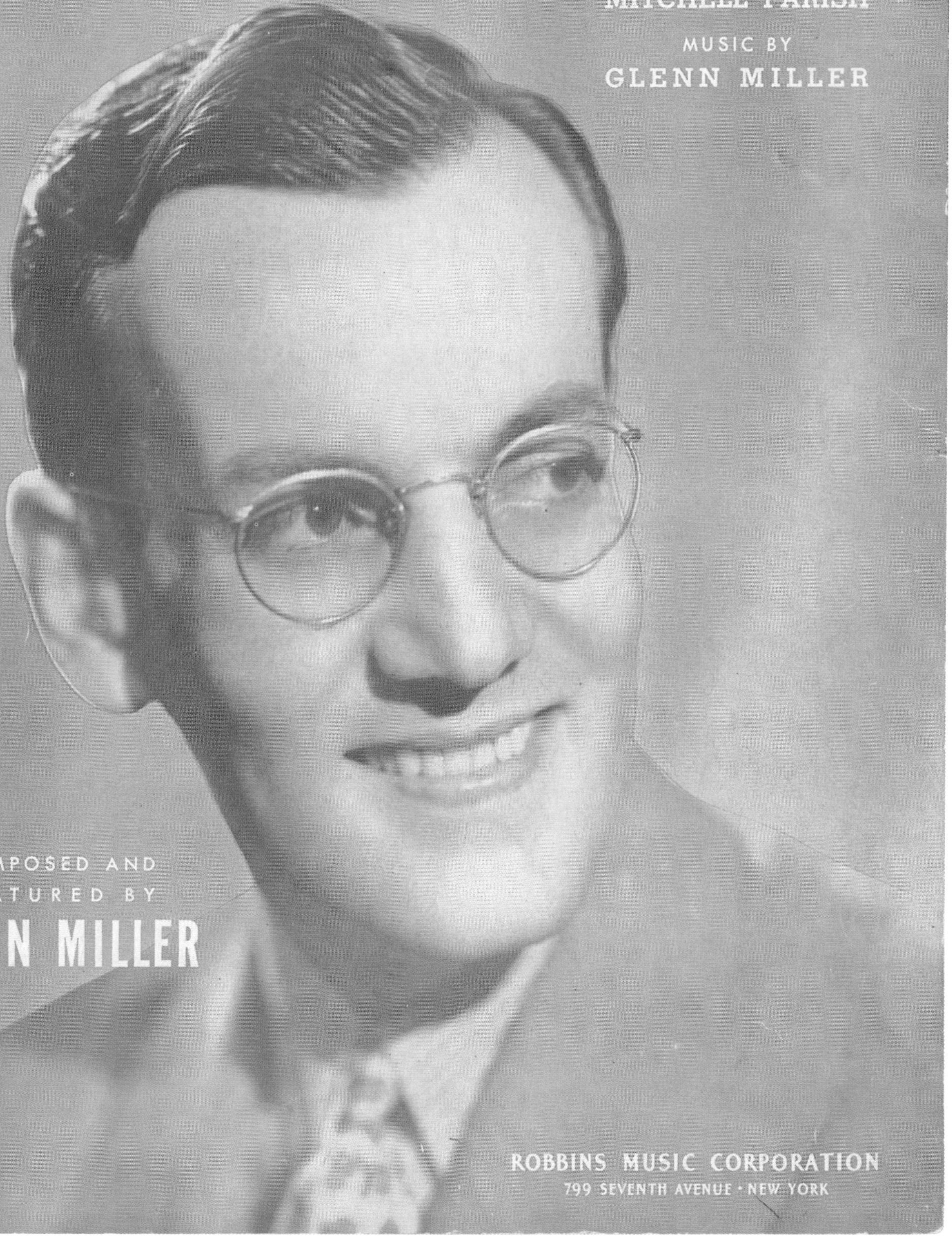

COMPOSED AND
FEATURED BY
GLENN MILLER

ROBBINS MUSIC CORPORATION
799 SEVENTH AVENUE · NEW YORK

Moonlight Serenade

Music by GLENN MILLER

I stand____ at your gate____ and the song that I sing is of moon-light, I

stand____ and I wait____ for the touch of your hand in the June night The

ros- es are sigh-ing a Moon-light Ser - e -nade, The

Moonlight Serenade

stars_____ are a - glow_____ and to - night. how their light_ sets me dream ing, My

love,_____ do you know_____ that your eyes_ are the stars_ brightly beam ing? I

bring you and sing you a Moon-light Ser - e - nade.

Let us stray till break of day in love's val-ley of dreams, Just

Moonlight Serenade

Belle of the Ball

Music by LEROY ANDERSON

Danc - ing so light - ly and smil - ing so bright - ly, To -

night you're the Belle of the Ball.

Is it a won - der the whole world is un - der the

Belle of the Ball

Belle of the Ball

So have a gay time, the mu-sic of May-time will end with the break of the dawn,_____ You and your laugh-ter will lin-ger long af-ter the sound of the mu-sic is gone,_____

Belle of the Ball

I will re - mem - ber the night   You were the

fair - est of all, _____ In my heart you'll be

danc - ing For - ev - er and ev - er the Belle of the

Ball. ____

f

ff

THE SYNCOPATED CLOCK

Words by
MITCHELL PARISH
Music by
LEROY ANDERSON

1619 BROADWAY, NEW YORK, N.Y.

The Syncopated Clock

Music by LEROY ANDERSON

There was a man like you and me,— as sim-ple as a
ex-perts came to hear and see,— But none of them could

man could ev-er be; And he was hap-py as a king,— ex-cept for one pe-
solve the mys-ter-y, They called Pro-fes-sor Ein-stein too,— He said "There's nothing

cul-iar thing. He had a clock that worked all right,— It worked all right, but
I can do." But soon the fick-le hu-man race— will find an-oth-er

The Syncopated Clock

not ex-act ly quite; In - stead of go-ing "tick tock, tick," the cra - zy clock went "tock, tick, tock." The
freak to take its place, And one fine day the man will hock that poor old Syn co - pa -ted Clock.

poor old man just raved and raved,— be - cause nobod - y could say why his sil-ly

clock be haved— that hick o - ry dick - o-ry way. But now a famous man is he,— He

owns a pub-lic cu - ri-os- i - ty; From far and wide the peo-ple flock— To hear The Syn-co-

The Syncopated Clock

pa -ted Clock. Tick- a - tock, tick-a - tock, There's a zing in the swing of that

clock, Tock-a - tick, tock-a - tick, Don't you think it's a mar- vel ous

trick? Ting-a - ling, ting-a - ling, There's a zong in the bong of that ring, Ling- a -

ting, ling-a - ting, Don't you think it's a won der-ful thing? The

Costume IV: *Manhattan Mary*; Majestic Theater, New York, 1927

Take Me in Your Arms

Music by FRED MARKUSH

Take Me in Your Arms

glad - ness_____ That we knew in the past,_____ One mo-ment's

mad - ness,_____ Al-though it be the last, hold me fast.

Blind me with your charms,___ With all the stardust in the sky,___ Take me in your arms___

And then good - bye

And then good - bye.

Ciao, Ciao, Bambina

Music by DOMENICO MODUGNO

Ciao, Ciao, Bam

bi - na, _____ the rain is fall - ing, _____

Once more I kiss you _____ and then good -

Ciao, Ciao, Bambina

bye._____ Our love was just like_____

a fair - y sto - ry,_____ But all its

glo - ry_____ must pass us by._____

Are rain - drops trem - bling_____ up - on your

Ciao, Ciao, Bambina

face, dear,_____ Or are they tear - drops_____ for the love we

knew?_____ Ciao, Ciao, Bam -bi - na,_____ my heart is

call - ing_____ While rain is fall - ing_____

___ I cry with you._____

Sleigh Ride

Music by LEROY ANDERSON

Just hear those sleigh bells jin-gle-ing, ring-ting-tin-gle-ing, too,____

Come on, it's love-ly weath-er for a sleigh ride to-geth-er with

you,____ Out-side the snow is fall-ing and

Sleigh Ride

friends are call - ing "Yoo hoo," _____ Come on, it's

love - ly weath - er for a sleigh ride to - geth - er with you. _____ Gid - dy -

up, gid - dy - up, gid - dy - up, let's go, Let's look at the

show, We're rid - ing in a won - der - land of

Sleigh Ride

snow. Gid - dy - up, gid-dy-up, gid-dy-

up, it's grand, Just hold-ing your hand, We're glid - ing a -

long with a song of a win-ter-y fair-y- land, Our cheeks are

nice and ros-y, and com-fy co-zy are we, We're snug-gled

Sleigh Ride

up to-geth-er like two birds of a feath-er would be._____ Let's take that

road be-fore us and sing a chor-us or two,_____ Come on, it's

love-ly weath-er for a sleigh ride to-geth-er with you._____ There's a

2. Last Time

you_____

mf dim   *p*   *f Fine*

Sleigh Ride

Interlude

birth-day par-ty at the home of Farm - er Gray, It-'ll

be the per-fect end-ing of a per - fect day, We'll be

sing-ing the songs we love to sing with-out a sin-gle stop, At the

legato

fi-re-place while we watch the chest-nuts pop. Pop! Pop! Pop! There's a

Sleigh Ride

hap- py feel- ing   noth- ing in the   world   can   buy,   When they

pass a- round the   cof- fee and the   pump - kin   pie,   It - 'll

near- ly be like a   pic- ture print by   Cur- ri - er and   Ives,

These won- der- ful   things are the things we re - mem- ber all thru our   lives! Just hear those

D.S. al Fine

123

A Little Bit Older

Music by JOE HARNELL

A Little Bit Older

sav - ing them all for the right man._____ E - ven

though it may take years_____ I'll

know when he ap - pears I'll be a

lit - tle bit old - er___ a lit - tle bit wis - er___ I

A Little Bit Older

won't wear my heart on my sleeve an - y - more. A

lit - tle bit long - er Lone - ly I'll be And

rit.

Then one fine day He'll come my way The man who will

real - ly love me.

Ruby

Music by HEINZ ROEMHELD

They say, Ru-by, you're like a dream, not al-ways what you seem,_____ and tho' my heart may break when I a-wake,___ let it be so,___ I on-ly know, Ru-by it's you.___ They

Ruby

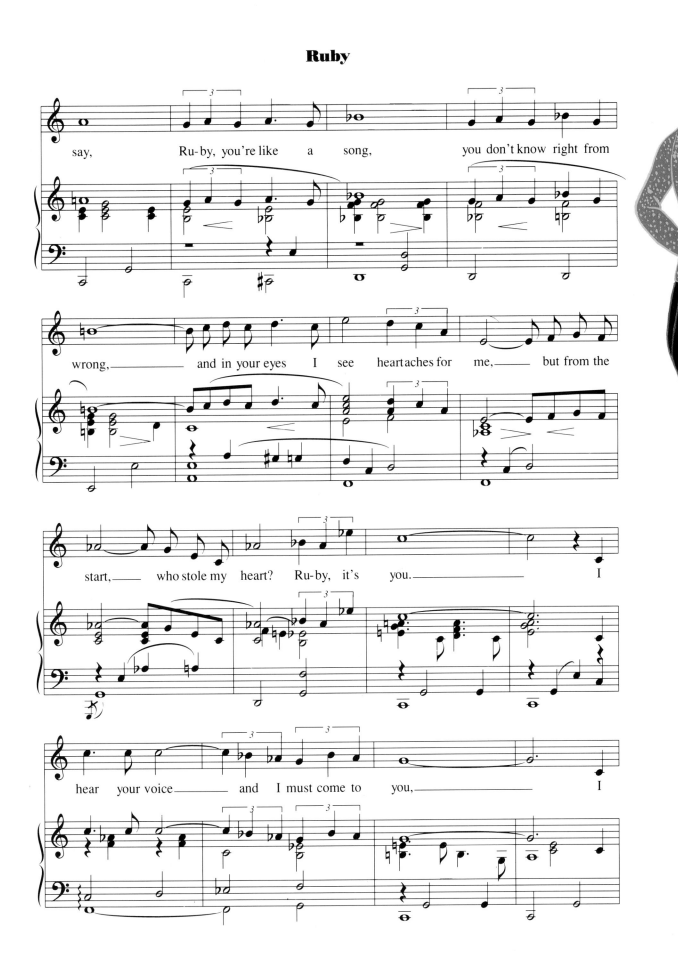

say, Ru-by, you're like a song, you don't know right from

wrong,_____ and in your eyes I see heartaches for me,_____ but from the

start,_____ who stole my heart? Ru-by, it's you._____ I

hear your voice_____ and I must come to you,_____ I

Ruby

have no choice,_____ what else can I do?_____ They

say, Ru-by, you're like a flame, in-to my life you came,_____

and tho' I should be-ware still I don't care,_____ you thrill me so,_____ I on-ly

know, Ru-by, it's you,_____ They you._____

Star Dust

Words by
MITCHELL PARISH

Music by
HOAGY CARMICHAEL

PUBLISHED FOR

VOCAL SOLO	.50
PIANO SOLO	.60
PIANO DUET (Arr. by Morton Gould)	.75
TWO PIANOS - FOUR HANDS (Arr. by Merkur)	1.00
PIANO ACCORDION	.50
GUITAR SOLO (Arr. by Cosmo)	.40

CHORAL EDITIONS

WOMEN'S VOICES - duet (S.A.)	.15
WOMEN'S VOICES (S.S.A.)	.15
MIXED QUARTET (S.A.T.B.)	.15
MALE QUARTET (T.T.B.B.)	.15
FULL ORCHESTRATION (Arr. by Henry Sopkin)	3.50
CONCERT ORCHESTRATION (Arr. by Henry Sopkin)	5.00
DANCE ORCHESTRATION	.75
VIOLIN CELLO AND PIANO	.60
VIOLIN SOLO (Transcrip. by Dave Rubinoff)	.60
FULL BAND (Arr. by Paul Yoder)	3.50
SYMPHONIC BAND (Arr. by Paul Yoder)	5.00
BAND	1.00
STRING CHOIR (Arr. by Morton Gould)	1.50
STRING SEXTET	1.00
WOODWIND SEXTET	1.00

STUDENT SERIES

TRUMPET SOLO (Including 2nd Trumpet and Piano Accompaniment)	.25
SAXOPHONE SOLO (Eb Solo with Bb Part and Piano Accompaniment)	.25
HAWAIIAN GUITAR or ELECTRIC HAWAIIAN GUITAR (With Spanish Guitar Acc.)	.25
SPANISH GUITAR (With Spanish Guitar Acc.)	.25
TROMBONE SOLO or DUET (With Piano Acc.)	.25
VIOLIN SOLO or DUET (With Piano Acc.)	.25
CLARINET SOLO or DUET (With Piano Acc.)	.25

Mills Music, Inc.
1619 BROADWAY, NEW YORK 19, N. Y.
MADE IN U.S.A.

Star Dust

Music by HOAGY CARMICHAEL

And now the pur-ple dusk of twi-light time Steals a-cross the mead-ows of my heart.

High up in the sky the lit-tle stars climb, Al-ways re-mind-ing me that we're a-part.

You wandered down the lane and far a-way. Leaving me a song that will not die.

Star Dust

Love is now the star dust of yes-ter-day, The mu-sic of the years gone by.

Some times I won-der why I spend the lone-ly night Dreaming of a song. The

mel-o-dy haunts my rev-er-ie, And I am once a-gain with you. When our

love was new, and each kiss an in-spir-a-tion, But that was long a-go: now

Star Dust

134

Costume, "New York": *American Millionairess*, Femina Theater, Paris. 1917

Forgotten Dreams

Music by LEROY ANDERSON

They keep re-turn-ing   Thru years of yearn-ing

No mat-ter how you try,   For-got-ten dreams won't die

You think it's o-ver   For-ev-er o-ver,

Forgotten Dreams

And then a voice will sigh, "For - got - ten dreams won't die."

Some - where in a crowd ed place Tho' she is - n't there you will see her face

Some - where you will hear her name, and sud - den- ly you know that the

thrill is still the same. You're still re - mem- ber-ing the thrill.

Forgotten Dreams

One day you loved her, One day you lost her

And now you won-der why For-got-ten tears won't dry

They keep re-turn - ing The flame still burn - ing

Tho' love has said good-bye, For-got-ten dreams won't die.

Mitchell Parish

As a youngster, Mitchell Parish came up from Shreveport, Louisiana, to the Lower East Side of New York. He received his early education in the public schools and on the sidewalks of Manhattan, and eventually was graduated summa cum laude from New York University, earning a Phi Beta Kappa key in his junior year. His plans for a career in medicine, and later in law, were abandoned when he was signed as a staff writer by a major music publisher. For decades, Mitchell Parish has been recognized internationally as a lyricist. He has written lyrics for more than four hundred songs, collaborating with many of the leading composers of popular music in America, including Duke Ellington, Hoagy Carmichael, Glenn Miller, and Leroy Anderson.

Erté

Born into an ancient Russian family, Romain de Tirtoff (his pen name, Erté, comes from the French pronunciation of his initials, R.T.) spent his first nineteen years in imperial St. Petersburg. In 1912 he went to Paris, where he was hired by the couturier Poiret. A few years later he began twenty-two years of designing covers for *Harper's Bazaar*, in a style that later came to be known as Art Deco. During this time — diversifying into the wide variety of artistic activities for which he became famous — he designed clothes for fashionable women, and for Hollywood stars such as Norma Shearer and Joan Crawford, and costumes and sets for *George White's Scandals*, the Folies-Bergère, the Paris Opera, and many other theatrical productions. At seventy-five, Erté began creating the graphics that led to yet another round of international acclaim. This was followed by excursions into new mediums, including sculpture, ceramics, and glass. His success has brought forth many books on his work: *Erté at Ninety* and *Erté at Ninety-five*, on his graphics, and *Erté Sculpture*. In 1989 he published an autobiography, *My Life/My Art*.

INDEX OF SONGS

INDEX OF COMPOSERS

The preparation of this book would not have been possible without the cooperation and generosity of the following: Mitchell Parish and Erté, of course; Eric Estorick and Sevenarts Ltd., who made it possible to reproduce the works of Erté; Paul Gottlieb and the staff of Harry N. Abrams, Inc., whose support was indispensable; Richard Smith, who supplied sheet music covers from his collection; Burton Litwin, who guided us expertly and wisely in business matters musical; Lourdes Richter and CPP Belwin, Inc., who graciously gave permission to reprint the music; Mark Nadler, who worked hard on the music transcriptions; Adobe Systems, Inc., which supplied typeface software for the lyrics; Coda Music Software, Inc., which supplied music software for the transcriptions; Charles May Reproductions, which set the type; Fulvio Nembrini and the staff of Arti Grafiche Motta, who printed the book when and how we wanted it; Clive Giboire and ISCOA, who made the color separations; Joseph Holloway of Louise Westergaard Productions, who helped in many ways; and, most especially, Louise Westergaard, the muse of *Stardust*.